My Polish family history

Vic Parker

Heinemann

young Explorer

www.heinemann.co.uk/library
Visit our website to find out more information about Heinemann Library books.

To order:
☎ Phone 44 (0) 1865 888066
🖹 Send a fax to 44 (0) 1865 314091
🖥 Visit the Heinemann Bookshop at www.heinemann.co.uk/library to browse our catalogue and order online.

First published in Great Britain by Heinemann Library, Halley Court, Jordan Hill, Oxford OX2 8EJ, part of Harcourt Education. Heinemann is a registered trademark of Harcourt Education Ltd.

Editorial: Charlotte Guillain
Design: Joanna Hinton-Malivoire
Picture research: Erica Martin
Production: Duncan Gilbert
Illustrated by Jacqueline McQuade
Originated by Modern Age
Printed and bound in China by South China Printing Co. Ltd.

ISBN 978 0 4310 1500 2 (hardback)
ISBN 978 0 4310 1505 7 (paperback)

12 11 10 09 08
10 9 8 7 6 5 4 3 2 1

British Library Cataloguing in Publication Data
Parker, Vic
My Polish family history. - (Family histories)
305.9'06912
A full catalogue record for this book is available from the British Library.

Acknowledgements
The publishers would like to thank the following for permission to reproduce photographs:
© Anthony Blake Photo Library p. **23** (Oceania News and Features); © Getty Images pp. **8** (Hulton Archive/Topical Press Agency), **16** (Hulton Archive), **19**, **27** (Hulton Archive/Fox Photos), **24** (Taxi/Barry Willis); © John James p. **20** (Alamy); © Lonely Planet Images pp. **9** (Jonathan Smith), **10** (Jeff Greenberg); © popperfoto.com p. **11**; © Courtsey of Zofia Scholtz p. **15**; © Victor Temin pp. **12** , **26** (Slava Katamidze Collection/Getty Images)

Cover photograph of girl at beach reproduced with permission of © Punchstock (Uppercut Images/Nick Tresidder).

Every effort has been made to contact copyright holders of any material reproduced in this book. Any omissions will be rectified in subsequent printings if notice is given to the publishers.

Contents

Words appearing in the text in bold, **like this**, are explained in the Glossary.

Ania's family history

My name is Ania. I am ten years old.
I live with my mother, father, and two
older brothers in a city called Coventry.

Coventry is in
the Midlands
in England.

Poland is in Eastern Europe, near Germany, the Czech Republic, Slovakia, Ukraine, Belarus, and Lithuania.

My family comes from a country called Poland. It has many forests, mountains, lakes, and rivers. It is very cold there in the winter.

My family tree

My mother's parents

Jan Rakowski
(my grandfather)
born 1908

Magda Zarebianka
(my grandmother)
born 1920

My father's parents

Frederyk Gabszewicz
(my grandfather)
born 1925

Barbara Kowalewna
(my grandmother)
born 1928

My grandparents grew up in Poland. One of my grandfathers was called Jan Rakowski. He was born in the city of Lwow (you say *Luh-vov*).

My grandfather had an older brother and sister. Their father was a teacher. Their mother looked after the family. They all lived in a small **apartment** with a kitchen, a living room, and two bedrooms.

Over the years, the borders of Poland have changed. Lwow is now in Ukraine and is called Lviv.

When my grandfather was six years old, a war started. It was called **World War One**. First Russian soldiers marched into Poland, then German soldiers. It was a frightening time.

My grandfather saw many Russian soldiers during the war.

Most people in Poland are Catholic. Catholics are **Christians**.

My grandfather was **Catholic**. He and the family went to church every Sunday and on special holy days. They often prayed at home, too.

My grandfather worked hard at school and he did well. Then he went to the university in Lwow. He studied to be a doctor. In his spare time he liked going to the theatre and music concerts, and walking in the park.

The theatres in Lwow are beautiful. This is the inside of the Opera House.

Millions of people died during World War Two.

My grandfather became a doctor in the Polish army. When he was thirty, the German army marched into Poland. This started a war called **World War Two**.

The Russian army seized parts of Poland too. The armies were cruel to the Polish people and made life very hard. My grandfather was taken away to a prison camp in Russia.

The Russian army destroyed many Polish towns.

After two years, my grandfather was allowed to leave Russia. He went back to join the Polish army. This was in Italy, helping the British army. My grandfather fell in love with a nurse called Magda and they got married.

An army hospital set up near the fighting is called a field hospital.

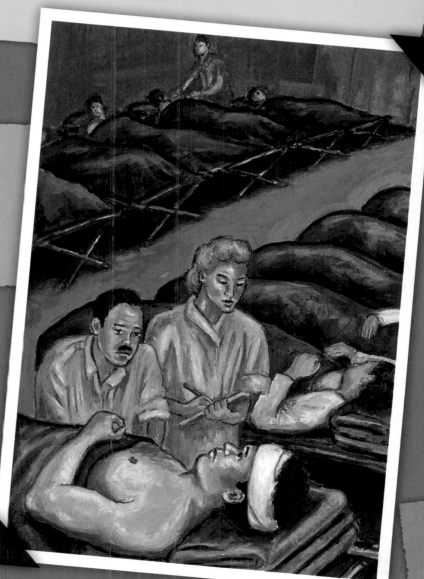

At the end of the war my grandfather wanted to return to Lwow, but he could not. It had been taken over by the **Soviet Union**, like many other Polish cities, towns and villages. My grandfather's home and job were gone.

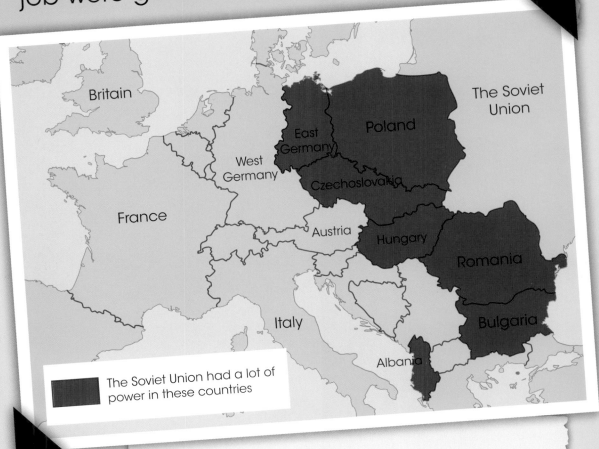

The Soviet Union had a lot of power in these countries

About half of Poland became part of the Soviet Union. Millions of Polish people could no longer live there.

After **World War Two**, thousands of Polish families came to make new lives in Britain.

My grandfather and grandmother went to Britain on a ship. They were taken to live in an empty army camp in Gloucestershire. The British government had opened up several camps like this for homeless Polish people.

At first my grandparents lived in the old soldiers' **barracks**. Everyone had to share cold, uncomfortable **dormitories** and bathrooms. Then my grandparents found work at the local hospital. They rented their own flat in a nearby town.

It was hard living in the camp, but the children still found ways to have fun. These children are having a race in traditional Polish clothes.

My family tree

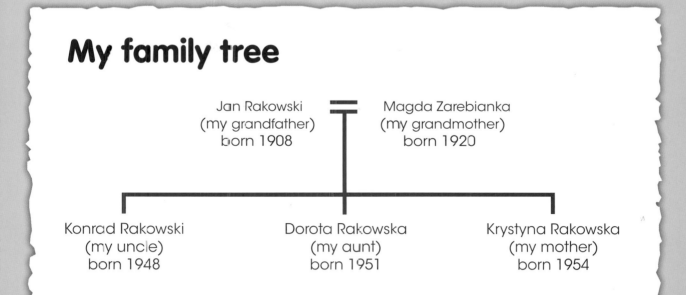

Jan Rakowski
(my grandfather)
born 1908

Magda Zarebianka
(my grandmother)
born 1920

Konrad Rakowski
(my uncle)
born 1948

Dorota Rakowska
(my aunt)
born 1951

Krystyna Rakowska
(my mother)
born 1954

Over the next few years, my grandparents had three children. My mother, Krystyna, grew up learning two languages. She spoke Polish at home, but she spoke English at school. When she was old enough, she studied to become a nurse like my grandmother.

Polish people call New Year's Eve *Sylwester*.

My mother had lots of Polish friends, because my grandparents kept in touch with many families from the camp. They often got together for parties. At one New Year's Eve party, my mother met a young man called Piotr.

Piotr was an **electrician**. His parents were Polish too. They had also come to England after the war. They lived in Coventry, where lots of other Polish people had settled.

During **World War Two**, Coventry was very heavily bombed by the German **air force**.

I see my grandparents on my father's side quite often, because they live near us in Coventry.

My brothers and I speak English at school. But we speak Polish with our parents and with our grandparents when we visit them. I like looking through old family photos with them.

At home, we eat mostly English food. But my mother cooks tasty Polish dishes for special occasions like Easter and Christmas. Beetroot soup is my favourite!

Food often used in Polish cooking includes sausage, fish, beetroot, cucumbers, potatoes, and sour cream.

I would like to visit Poland one day, to see what the country is like. But I want to stay living in Britain when I grow up. I would like to be on TV or maybe the radio.

There is a radio station in Coventry called "Poles Apart", which is especially for Polish people.

My new friends tell me about life in Poland and I tell them about life in Britain.

These days, more Polish people are coming to Britain to work. Some stay for a short while and others stay for good. Some Polish children have just joined my school so I have made new friends.

Then and now

My grandfather grew up during two world wars. He saw many soldiers in his city. I am growing up during a peaceful time.

Coventry was bombed during **World War Two**, and many buildings were destroyed. Today, Coventry has been built again. The ruins of the old cathedral are still standing.

Ania's family tree

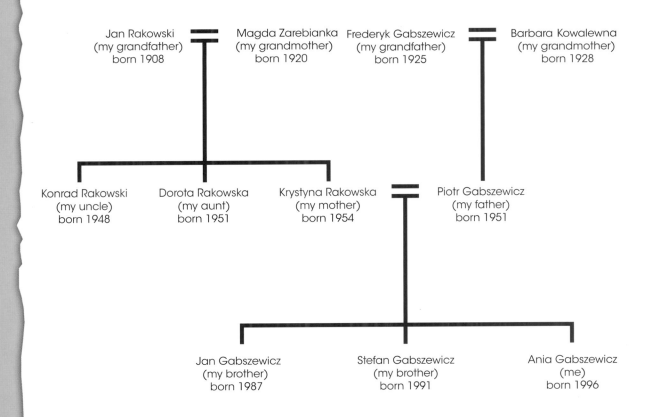

Jan Rakowski (my grandfather) born 1908

Magda Zarebianka (my grandmother) born 1920

Frederyk Gabszewicz (my grandfather) born 1925

Barbara Kowalewna (my grandmother) born 1928

Konrad Rakowski (my uncle) born 1948

Dorota Rakowska (my aunt) born 1951

Krystyna Rakowska (my mother) born 1954

Piotr Gabszewicz (my father) born 1951

Jan Gabszewicz (my brother) born 1987

Stefan Gabszewicz (my brother) born 1991

Ania Gabszewicz (me) born 1996

Finding out about your family history

- See if your family members have any photographs of when they got married, or when they were young. You could turn the photographs into a family history scrapbook. Get your family to write their memories next to the photographs.

- Ask your family about what life was like when they grew up. What toys did they like to play with? What food did they like to eat? What were their friends like? Did they go through difficult times? You could record them talking or write down what they tell you.

- Ask your mother, father, aunts, uncles, and grandparents to help you make your own family tree.

- Look at a map and draw circles around the places where your family has lived. Find out about those places through books and websites. See if your family can take you on trips there.

More books to read

A Picture of Grandmother, Esther Hautzig (Farrar Straus Giroux, 2002)

Flowers on the Wall, Miriam Nerlove (Atheneum Books for Young Readers, 1995)

Poland (Discovering Cultures), Sharon Gordon (Benchmark Books, 2004)

Websites

www.bbc.co.uk/history/walk/memory_index.shtml
This website gives you tips on finding out about your own family history.

http://pbskids.org/wayback/family/tree/index.html
This website helps you to put together your own family tree.

Glossary

air force soldiers are usually divided into an army who fights on land, a navy who fights at sea, and an air force who fight using aeroplanes

apartment home made up of rooms on one floor of a larger building

barracks building for soldiers to live in

Catholic type of Christian. Their leader is a man called the Pope who lives in Italy.

Christian person who follows the teachings of Jesus Christ in a book called the Bible

dormitory large bedroom shared by lots of people

electrician person whose job is to work with electricity

Soviet Union large country that was formed in 1922, made up of many smaller countries including Russia and Ukraine

World War One war that many countries fought in, which took place from 1914 to 1918

World War Two war that many countries fought in, which took place from 1939 to 1945

Index